THE OCEANS EXPLORED

OCEAN HABITAT

Claudia Martin

Illustrated by Fiona Osbaldstone

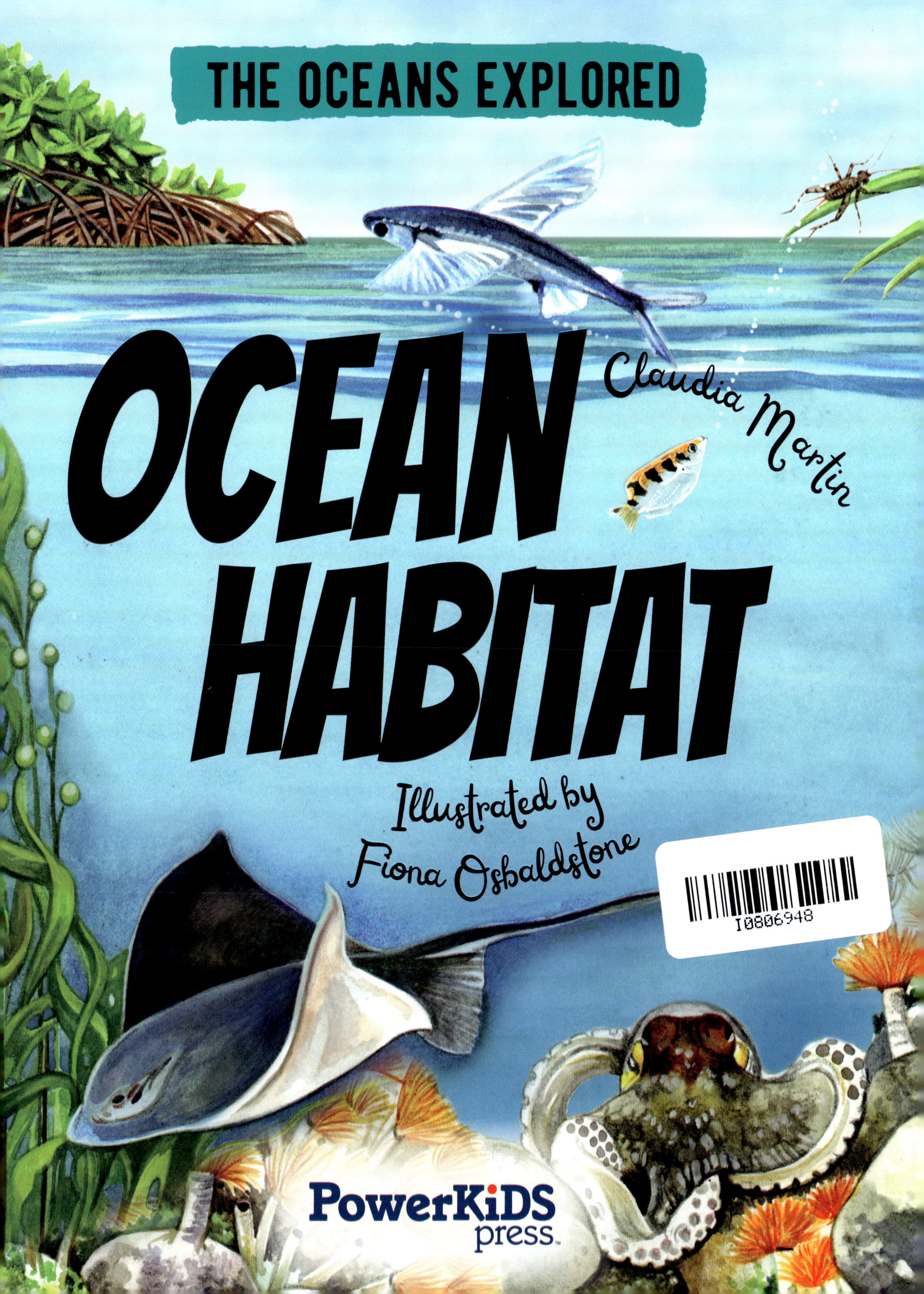

PowerKiDS press

Published in 2026
by The Rosen Publishing Group, Inc.
2544 Clinton Street, Buffalo, NY 14224

First published in 2021 in Great Britain by Wayland

Credits

Author and editor: Claudia Martin
Illustrator: Fiona Osbaldstone
Designer: Clare Nicholas
Proofreader: Annabel Savery

The publisher would like to thank the following for permission to reproduce their photographs:
Alamy: NOAA 4l, Seaphotoart 9, Photography by Marco 10, Edward Rowland 20, David Shale/Nature Picture Library 27, David R. Frazier Photolibrary, Inc. 28; Getty Images: Jan Abadschieff 15, Georgette Douwma 16, Michael Zeigler/iStock 19; Shutterstock: Tarpan 4r, Ondrej Prosicky 5tl, Damsea 5tr and 13, Rich Carey 5b, JaklZdenek 7, Tomas Kotouc 23, FloridaStock 24.

Cataloging-in-Publication Data

Names: Martin, Claudia, author. | Osbaldstone, Fiona, illustrator.
Title: Ocean habitat / by Claudia Martin, illustrated by Fiona Osbaldstone.
Description: Buffalo, NY : PowerKids Press, 2026. | Series: The oceans explored | Includes glossary and index.
Identifiers: ISBN 9781499453973 (pbk.) | ISBN 9781499453980 (library bound) | ISBN 9781499453997 (ebook)
Subjects: LCSH: Marine ecology--Juvenile literature. | Ocean--Juvenile literature.
Classification: LCC QH541.5.S3 M378 2026 | DDC 577.7--dc23

Manufactured in the United States of America

CPSIA Compliance Information: Batch #CSPK26. For further information contact Rosen Publishing at 1-800-237-9932.

CONTENTS

OCEAN HABITATS

A living thing's natural home is its habitat. Animals, plants, and seaweeds are all suited to their habitat, where they usually find the light, warmth, food, and shelter they need. Today, all ocean habitats are in danger from pollution and rising temperatures. When a habitat is damaged, all its living things are at risk.

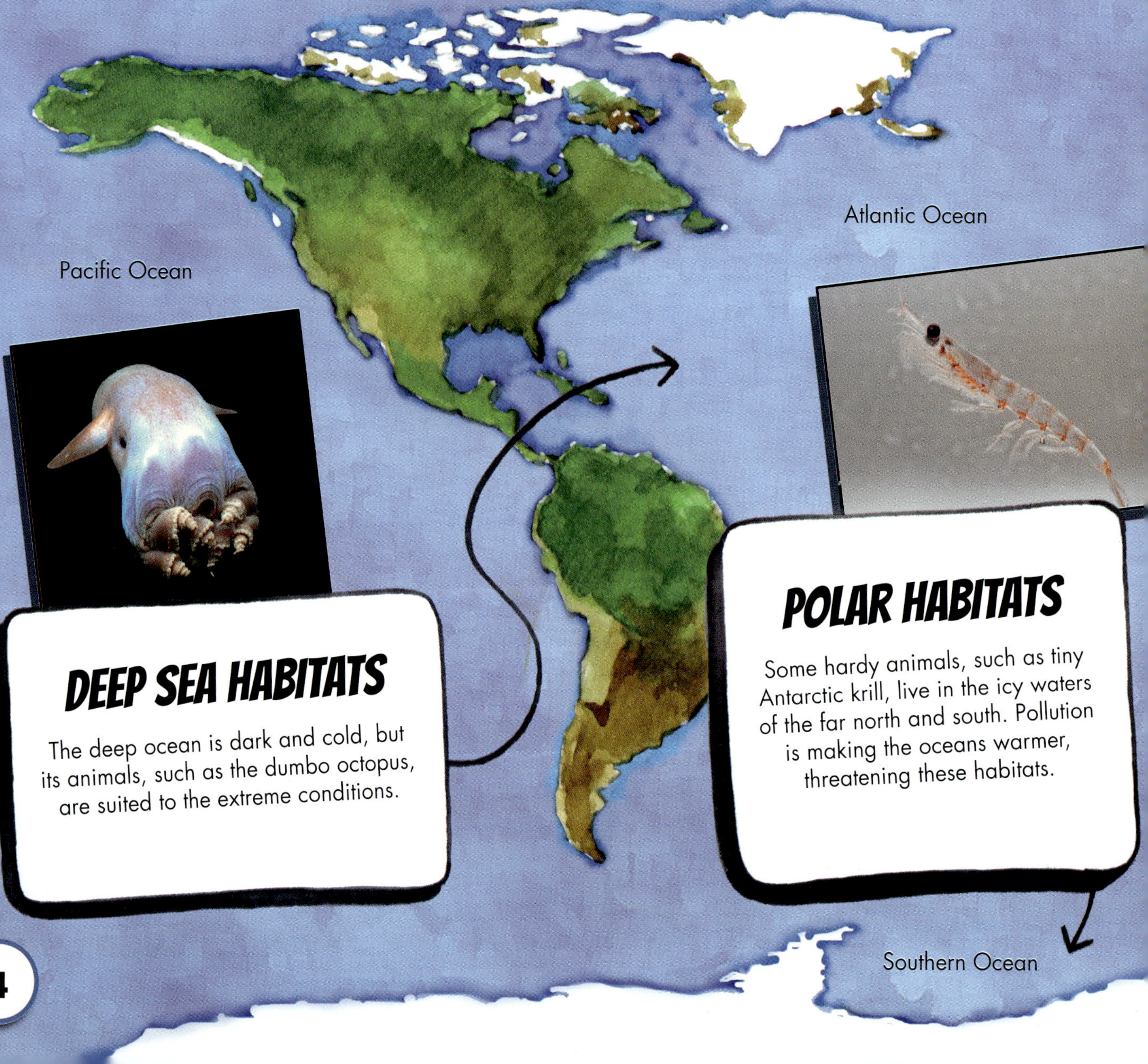

DEEP SEA HABITATS

The deep ocean is dark and cold, but its animals, such as the dumbo octopus, are suited to the extreme conditions.

POLAR HABITATS

Some hardy animals, such as tiny Antarctic krill, live in the icy waters of the far north and south. Pollution is making the oceans warmer, threatening these habitats.

COASTAL HABITATS

Where the land meets the sea, the ocean may crash against cliffs or flow through mangrove forests. Coastal habitats are particularly at risk of pollution from cities and factories.

SHALLOW WATER HABITATS

Close to land, the water is warmed and brightly lit by sunlight, giving life to plants and corals. If these growing things are disturbed, the animals they shelter may die.

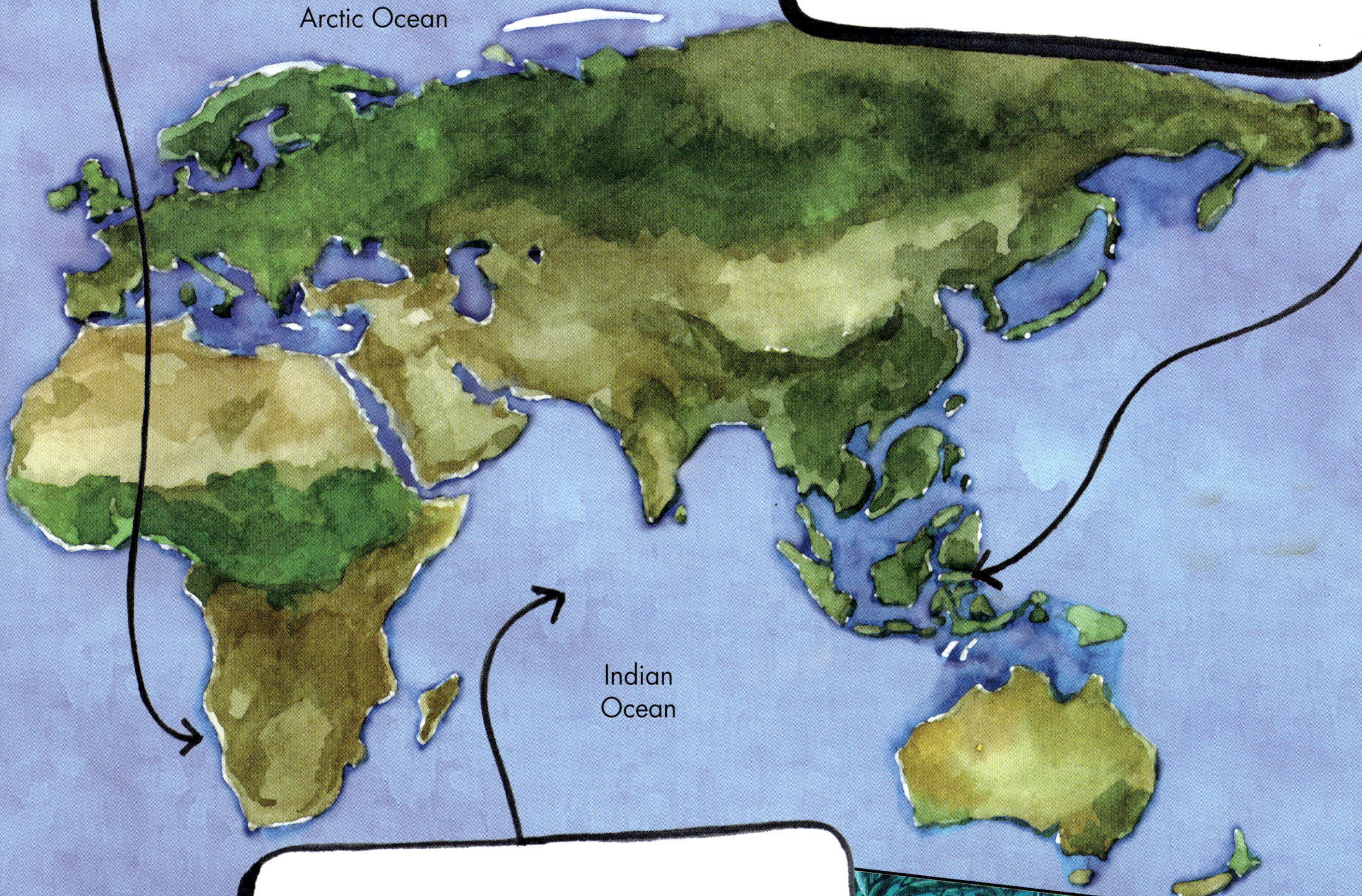

OPEN OCEAN HABITATS

Far from land, whales, sharks and shoals of fish speed along. Even here, the water may be at risk of being polluted by plastic and factory waste.

ON THE SHORE

Waves may break against tall, rocky cliffs or on a sandy or muddy beach.

Each of these habitats is home to a different group of living things.

Seabirds, such as puffins, land on cliffs to rest and to build their nests. High on rocky ledges, their eggs and chicks are out of reach of most predators. Puffins spend the rest of their time diving into the ocean to catch small fish, such as sandeels.

Beaches are challenging habitats for animals and plants. The rising and falling of the daily tides floods the beach then exposes it to wind and sun. Some animals, such as hard-shelled mussels and limpets, attach themselves to rocks so they are not pulled out to sea. Tiny sand hoppers, which are related to crabs, bury themselves beneath the damp sand, coming out when the tide is low to feed on seaweed.

Atlantic puffins rest on the cliffs of Scotland before diving into the ocean in pursuit of small fish.

ROCK POOLS

Hollows in seaside rocks are filled with water when the tide is high.

When the tide goes out, a pool of water is left behind.

Shallow rock pools may dry out completely when the tide goes out. Animals, plants, and plant-like algae must survive being covered by water then drying in the baking sun or fierce blasts of wind. Tough-skinned starfish are common rock pool animals, able to survive short periods out of water. They crawl across the rock in search of prey using the sticky suckers on the undersides of their arms.

The starburst anemone looks like a flower, but is an animal with stinging tentacles. It attaches itself to rocks in pools. When the tide is out, it hides beneath the gravel and seashells that stick to its tentacles. If a different type of anemone enters its pool, the starburst stings until it moves away.

On the coast of France, a Mediterranean red starfish clings to the walls of a rock pool.

A young black-winged stilt searches for insects in the shallow water of an Australian salt marsh.

SALT MARSHES

Salt marshes are found on low, coastal land that is flooded at high tide.

Growing here are land plants, such as samphire, that can survive in saltwater.

Many fish and birds lay their eggs in salt marshes. Plants here act as shelter from predators for baby fish. Adult birds also live on marshes, hunting for fish in the shallow water or for insects on plants. Many of these birds, such as the black-winged stilt, have long legs so they can wade easily. Crabs are common in this habitat, tunnelling into the soft mud for safety.

Like all coastal habitats, salt marshes are at risk from pollution from factories, which damages plants and animals. Across the world, marshes are shrinking or disappearing. People have reclaimed many marshes from the sea, building up the land above sea level so it can be used as farmland or for building.

MANGROVE FORESTS

Unlike most trees, mangroves live in saltwater, their stilt-like roots keeping their leaves above the tide.

Mangrove forests are found along tropical coasts.

This habitat is a meeting place of land and sea, where leaves dangle over saltwater. The banded archerfish makes use of this closeness. It sucks in water then spits jets at insects crawling on branches. The insects are knocked into the water, then eaten. Birds, such as the mangrove pitta, swoop from their tree perches to catch small crabs and snails.

Mangroves are important habitats because they are fish nurseries. Here eggs are laid and fish grow until they are big enough to swim out to sea. Mangroves also form a barrier that protects towns from ocean floods. Yet a fifth of mangrove forests have been cut down.

In the warm waters of the Caribbean Sea, a mangrove forest shelters shoals of darting fish.

SEAGRASS MEADOWS

Seagrasses are plants that grow on the seabed.

Like all plants, they make their food from sunlight, so they live in shallow, sunlit water.

Seagrass meadows are found close to the shore in all the world's oceans, apart from around the coasts of Antarctica in the cold Southern Ocean. Seagrasses are at risk from chemicals that are washed into the water from farms and factories. These plants, and the animals that live among them, are also disturbed by building, fishing, and motorboating.

Seagrasses are food for many animals, from green turtles to manatees. Manatees are plant-eating mammals that are distantly related to elephants. The meadows are also shelter for fish hiding from predators or watching for prey. The leafy seadragon does both, its color and shape camouflaging it among the grasses.

Hiding among seagrass, a male leafy seadragon carries eggs on his tail to keep them safe until they hatch.

Panda butterflyfish swim over a coral reef off the coast of Thailand, in the western Pacific Ocean.

CORAL REEFS

In warm, shallow water, tiny animals called coral polyps build coral reefs.

Reefs are home to a quarter of all species of ocean animals.

Coral polyps build a hard skeleton around their soft body. Reefs are made of the skeletons of millions of polyps. Today, two-thirds of coral reefs are at risk as polyps are sensitive to rises in water temperature. The oceans are warming because of the gases released when humans burn fossil fuels in factories and vehicle engines. These gases trap heat around Earth, causing global warming.

Many coral reef fish are brightly colored and patterned. This helps to camouflage them on the colorful reef. Reef fish often have differently shaped bodies from fish that live in the open ocean. The bodies of reef fish are thin from side to side, a bit like pancakes. This helps them change direction swiftly, darting between corals to escape danger.

KELP FORESTS

Kelp forests grow in cool, coastal waters of every ocean except the Southern Ocean.

Some animals cling to the kelp, while others hunt for prey among its fronds.

Although kelp looks like a plant, it is an algae, which are simpler living things than plants. However, like a plant, kelp makes its own food from sunlight, in its green, leaf-like fronds. Since kelp is suited to cool water, rising sea temperatures are killing kelp forests in warmer regions. Kelp forests are spreading closer to the poles, into areas that were once too cold.

Kelp is food for crawling animals, such as sea snails, crabs, and sea urchins. These small creatures, as well as the fish that dart among the kelp, are food for larger animals, such as California sea lions and bat rays. Rays swim between the fronds by flapping their wing-like fins.

Close to the coast of California, in the Pacific Ocean, a sea lion plays in a kelp forest.

Half-buried in the seabed near the Indonesian island of Sulawesi, a sand striker waits for passing prey.

THE COASTAL SEABED

Close to the coast, the sloping seabed is busy with life.

Sand, mud, and rocks are hiding places or a surface to stick to.

Octopuses and eels hide among rocks as they wait for prey. Sea spiders crawl along on their eight legs, looking for sponges or corals to eat. Resting on the seafloor are sea cucumbers, which feed on tiny or rotting living things.

Many seabed animals are worms, which have a tube-like body and no arms, legs or eyes. Feather duster worms attach themselves to the seabed, catching food in their feathery tentacles. Other worms are burrowers. One of them is the sand striker, which can grow up to 10 feet (3 m) long. It hides under sand or mud, waiting for passing fish, which it senses with its feelers, called antennae. Then it strikes with its sharp jaws, which can slice prey in half.

THE OPEN OCEAN

The world's largest habitat is the open ocean, which covers nearly two-thirds of Earth's surface.

The open ocean is all the world's ocean that is neither near the coast nor the seabed.

No plants with roots can grow here, as the seabed is too far below. Yet drifting through the sunlit surface waters are simple rootless plants too small to be seen. These are food for little animals, such as krill, which are eaten by bigger animals, from squid to whales.

Since there are no hiding places in the open ocean, many animals rely on speed to escape predators. Speedy flying fish can even leap out of the water, gliding around 164 feet (50 m) through the air using their wing-like fins. Many open ocean fish are large, so only the biggest predators can attack them. After the huge sharks and rays, the ocean sunfish is the largest fish.
It grows up to 11 feet (3.3 m) long.

An ocean sunfish swims in the warm, sunlit surface waters of the Atlantic Ocean.

A polar bear mother and cub walk across the sea ice of the Arctic Ocean.

POLAR WATERS

The North Pole is in the Arctic Ocean, while the Southern Ocean surrounds Antarctica, where the South Pole is found.

Animals that live in polar waters have special features to help them survive the cold.

In winter, the surface of the Arctic Ocean and the sea surrounding Antarctica freezes. In summer, some of this sea ice melts. Sea ice is a key part of this habitat. The ice is a resting place for seals and seabirds. Polar bears hunt on the ice, waiting for seals to come up for air. Global warming is melting the ice a little more each year, putting these polar animals at risk.

All the mammals that swim in polar waters – including polar bears and whales, such as the long-tusked narwhal – have a thick layer of fat, called blubber, to keep in their body heat. Polar bears also have dense fur. Polar seabirds, such as penguins, have thick, waterproof feathers.

THE DEEP OCEAN

Sunlight cannot reach into the deep ocean, so no plants can grow.

In the cold and dark, a few animals survive by feeding on each other or on whatever sinks to the bottom.

In the darkness, some animals make their own light using special body parts. Some, such as dragonfish, dangle a light to attract prey. Others use light to get the attention of a mate. Many deep-sea fish have large eyes, so they can see in what little light there is.

Many deep-sea animals have huge mouths and stomachs so they can swallow any prey they come across. Some deep-sea animals are much bigger than relatives that live elsewhere. The giant isopod is related to woodlice, but grows up to 30 inches (76 cm) long. It crawls along looking for dead animals that have sunk to the seabed.

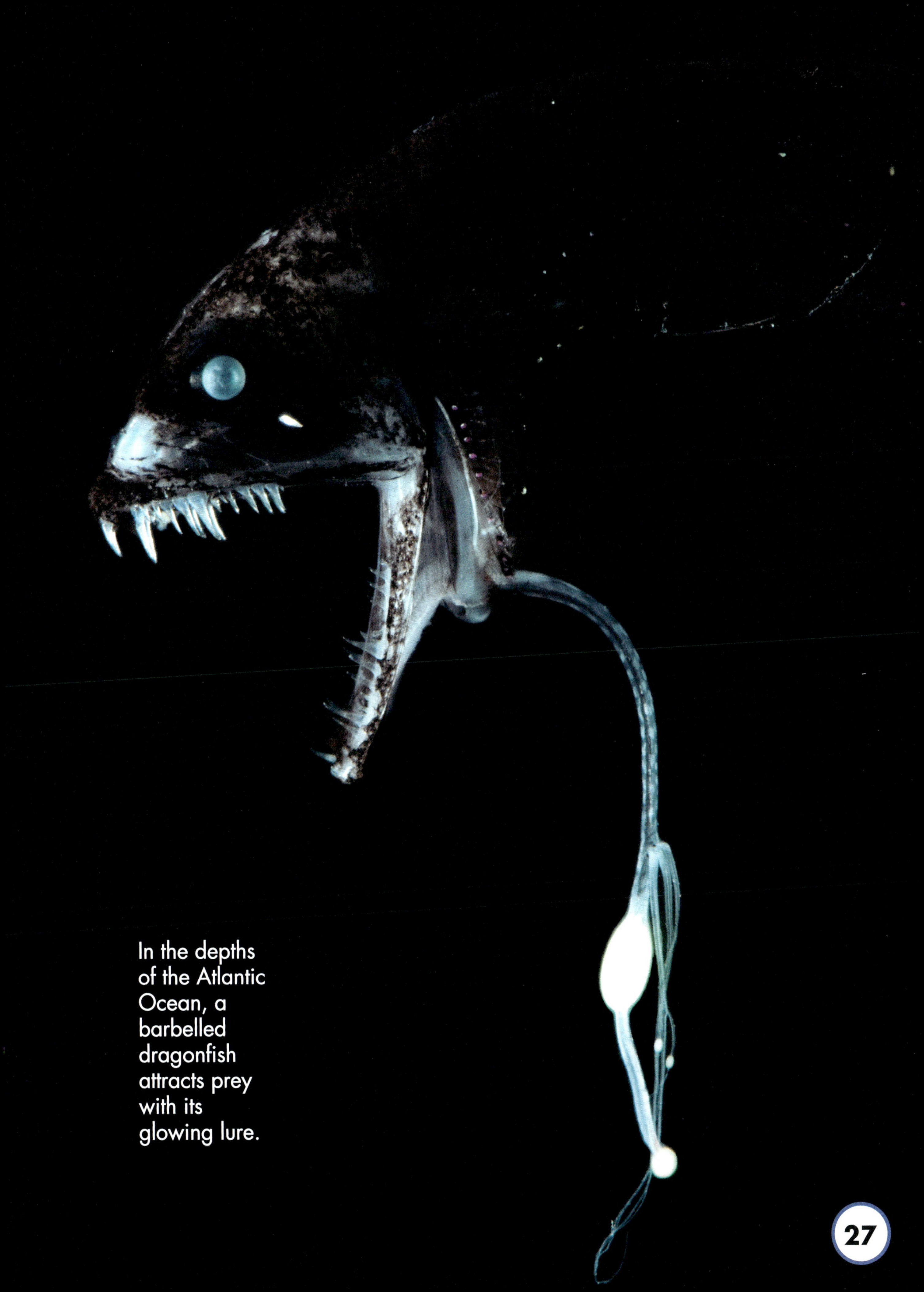

In the depths of the Atlantic Ocean, a barbelled dragonfish attracts prey with its glowing lure.

A park ranger and ocean scientists monitor the elephant seals in Año Nuevo State Park in California.

PROTECTING HABITATS

All the ocean's habitats need protection from pollution and destruction.

Governments, charities, and ordinary people are working to save them.

Many governments pass laws that stop factories and farms polluting the oceans. Charities ask governments to do more. Ordinary people should try to leave every habitat as they found it and never drop trash. Some people help out by organizing litter cleanups on local beaches. Everyone can try to make fewer car journeys, to burn less oil and slow global warming.

One way to save habitats is to protect particular areas by law, making it illegal to pollute them. There are now thousands of protected areas, from Australia's Great Barrier Reef Marine Park to Año Nuevo State Park, in the U.S. state of California, which is home to elephant seals. Parks are often patrolled by rangers in boats.

GLOSSARY

algae simple, plant-like living things

antennae long, thin feelers found on the heads of some animals

camouflage body colors and shapes that allow an animal to blend in with its surroundings

coastal near the coast, where the ocean meets the land

coral reef a stony underwater ridge made of the skeletons of millions of tiny animals called coral polyps

fin a flattened body part used for steering or swimming by fish and some other ocean animals

fossil fuels fuels formed over millions of years from the bodies of dead plants and animals

global warming the rising of the temperatures of Earth's air and oceans, caused largely by human activities

habitat the natural home of a group of animals and plants

hardy able to survive in difficult conditions

mammal an animal with hair; female mammals feed their babies milk

marsh low, wet land

mate a partner for making babies

oil a liquid fuel found inside Earth's rocks

plant a living thing that makes its own food from sunlight

pollution releasing harmful materials or energy into the ocean, air, or soil

predator an animal that eats other animals

prey an animal that is eaten by other animals

reclaim to dry out and put to use land that was previously underwater

saltwater ocean water, which contains salt and other minerals

seaweed plant-like algae that grows in the ocean or on the shore

shoal a group of fish swimming together

shore the land along the edge of the ocean

species a group of animals that look similar to each other and can make babies together

tentacle a bendy body part used for grasping or moving

tide the regular rising and falling of the oceans, caused by the pull of the Moon

tropical found in an area around the equator, where it is hot all year

FURTHER READING

Books

Habitats (Science Skills Sorted), Anna Claybourne (Franklin Watts, 2019)

Marine Biomes (Earth's Natural Biomes), Louise and Richard Spilsbury (Wayland, 2019)

Ocean: Secrets of the Deep, Sabrina Weiss (What on Earth Books, 2019)

The Ocean Is Kind of a Big Deal, Nick Seluk (Orchard Books, 2022)

Websites

Find out more about ocean habitats on these websites:

https://ocean.si.edu/ocean-life/plants-algae/seagrass-and-seagrass-beds

www.gbrmpa.gov.au

www.worldwildlife.org/habitats/ocean-habitat

INDEX